VINPOCETINE

Boost Your BRAIN POWER with Periwinkle Extract!

A Health Learning Handbook

Beth M. Ley, Ph.D.

BL Publications

Hanover, MN

BL Publications, Hanover, MN
1-877-BOOKS11
email: bley@blpublications.com

Library of Congress Cataloging-in-Publication Data

Ley, Beth M., 1964-
   Vinpocetine : revitalize your brain with periwinkle extract! / Beth M. Ley.-- 2nd ed.
       p. cm. -- (A health learning handbook)
   Includes bibliographical references (p.   ) and index.
   ISBN 1-890766-08-9
   1. Vinpocetine. I. Title. II. Series.
RM666.V56 L49 2000
615'.32393--dc21   99-050632

Printed in the United States of America

First edition: January 2000
Second edition: February 2008

This book is not intended as medical advise. Its purpose is solely educational. Please consult your health care professional for all health problems.

Credits:
Typesetting and Cover Design: BL Publications
Proofreading: Virginia Simpson-Magruder

This book is dedicated

to the loving memory of

Orion (Pete) Buttke

"Granpa"

Table of Contents

Health Learning Handbooks

Health Learning Handbooks are designed to provide interesting and useful information to improve one's health and well-being by learning what the body needs to obtain and maintain good health.

Good health should not be thought of as the absence of disease. We should avoid this negative, disease-orientated thinking and concentrate on what we must to do to remain healthy. Health results from supplying what is essential to the body on a daily basis, while disease results from living without what the body needs. We are responsible for our own health and should take control of it before disease does.

Our health depends on education. Education is power.

YOU NEED TO KNOW...
THE HEALTH MESSAGE

Do you not know that you are God's temple and that God's Spirit dwells in you? If anyone destroys God's temple, God will destroy him, For God's temple is holy and that temple you are.

1 Corinthians 3:16-17

So, whether you eat or drink, or whatever you do, do all to the glory of God.

1 Corinthians 10:31

Introduction

Are we all losing our minds?

When my grandfather died at the age of 95, he had lived a good and full life and he died in his sleep. What more could a person ask for, right? Well, for the last 5 or so years of his life, he experienced severe mental deterioration. The last time I went to visit him at the nursing home where he was staying in North Dakota, he did not know my name. I don't think he really even knew who I was. He could, however, relate detailed stories about the water wells he drilled throughout the North Dakota plains in the late 1920's and 1930's. He knew exactly where those wells were and probably what the lady of the house gave him for breakfast.

It is very difficult to witness someone lose their memory and just as difficult to experience it yourself. We don't know who will be affected and who will not, but statistics show that the frequency at which it is happening, is increasing.

As the average life expectancy continues to increase, it seems a shame if one cannot enjoy those extra years to the fullest. What is the point of living 90 or 100 years of age if you don't know who you are talking to and cannot function in society. Without a fully functioning brain, the quality of life will be nothing.

Nutritional and medical advisors tell people to exercise, eat right, take supplements, eat more fiber, avoid saturated fats, don't smoke, and various other ways to live longer healthier lives. Many people seem to be listening to such advice. As a result, average life spans have risen steadily, the incidence of heart disease is declining and certain cancer rates are dropping. The problem is that nursing homes are filling up with individuals who are no longer functioning mentally. In addition to taking care of our bodies, we need to take care of our brain. Senility is **not** a normal part of getting older.

Various botanicals have long been used to enhance our mental capacities. Vinpocetine (pronounced vin-poe-cee-tin) has many of the same cerebral-enhancing effects as another more well known botanical extract, ginkgo biloba, but is superior in some aspects. Vinpocetine is touted as an enhancer of both cerebral circulation and memory.

Vinpocetine is a derivative of vincamine, which is an alkaloid extracted from the periwinkle plant, used widely in Europe for geriatrics in the treatment of cerebral senility. Vinpocetine demonstrates many of the same benefits as vincamine, but in the United States, vinpocetine, is considered a plant derivative and is emerging as an ingredient in dietary supplements for brain/mind enhancement.

This is because supplement and drug laws and regulations vary from one country to another. For example, in Germany, St. John's Wort, now established as a beneficial aid in the treatment of mild to moderate depression, is prescribed by physicians (and reportedly out sells Prozac® in that country by a ratio of 25:1). Yet in the United States, St. John's Wort is sold over the counter as a a dietary supplement.

Vinpocetine has been used in clinical practice for over 20 years in Hungary and other countries for the treatment of cerebrovascular disorders and related symptoms. Vinpocetine, in addition to its therapeutic utilization, has become a reference compound in the pharmacological research of cognitive deficits. (Kiss)

Before continuing this discussion of vinpocetine, I want to provide you with some background information on the brain.

Our Control Center: The Brain

The brain is responsible for all of our internal functions, as well as our interactions with our external surroundings. In order to maintain this relationship, the brain must be functioning. Optimal functioning is desired for optimal interaction. In order for us to enjoy life to the fullest, we need to be in control.

As the control center of all physical and intellectual activity in the body, the brain is a delicate and complex structure. As many as 100 billion different cells, with millions and millions of neurons, form a seemingly innumerable number of connections.

Around the age of 30 neurons (brain cells) begin to die (or go dormant) at a faster rate than they are replaced, thus beginning the deteriorative process that becomes more and more obvious as we get older. In some people, for reasons we are only beginning to learn about, this process is far more evident than in others. Some octogenarians will be fully self sufficient, remembering not only what they need to pick up at the store that day, but the details of a family vacation 40 years ago, while others cannot remember their phone number, the names of their children, grandchildren, or what they had for supper the night before.

It is estimated by some authorities that more than 90% of long-term nursing home patients have a moderate to severe loss of intellectual function. (Mark)

Neurons are large cells which require huge amounts of energy and nutrition to function properly. The brain normally receives 15-20% of the body's total blood supply and uses 15-20% of the body's total inhaled oxygen. The brain uses this oxygen, along with glucose to produce and use 15-20% of the body's total ATP energy. Unlike most other cells, which can burn fat or sugar (glucose) for their energy needs, neurons can only burn glucose. Under normal conditions, they typically consume 50% of the total blood glucose.

Unlike liver and muscle cells, which can store large amounts of glucose as glycogen, neurons can only store, at most, a minute or two worth of glucose. Therefore, they are dependent upon a continuous and uninterrupted blood supply to maintain normal energy metabolism and avoid injury or death.

ATP-Producing Processes in Brain Cells

This glucose is used by neurons to produce energy. Under normal conditions of adequate oxygen supply, neurons convert glucose into adenosine triphosphate (ATP) through a three-phase process.

1. The first phase occurs in the cytoplasm of the cell (the gel-like stuff inside the cell membrane surrounding the nucleus and other organelles). It is called "aerobic glycolysis," as it involves oxygen. As each molecule of glucose is metabolized through aerobic glycolysis, two molecules of ATP are produced. In addition, two other by-products result that are used to make further ATP in the next two phases of energy production.

2. The by-product of aerobically burning glucose is pyruvic acid, which is then converted to acetyl-coenzyme A (ACoA).

3. ACoA is then metabolized through the Krebs (also known as the citric acid cycle) to generate more ATP. The Krebs cycle occurs inside the mitochondria, which are also known as the "power-producing plants" of the cell.

The other energy-rich substance produced through aerobic glycolysis is NADH – the active coenzyme of vitamin B3.

Aerobic glycolysis produces two molecules of NADH for each molecule of glucose burned. The NADH is then transported to the mitochondria, where it serves as a fuel in the third phase of energy metabolism – the electron transport side chain (ETSC).

Each NADH that runs through the ETSC, with adequate oxygen supplies, produces three molecules of ATP. With adequate oxygen, through the successful interaction of aerobic glycolysis, the Kreb's cycle, and the ETSC, a single molecule of glucose can yield up to 38 molecules of ATP.

When neurons are under-supplied with oxygen, however, anaerobic (without oxygen) glycolysis occurs. For each molecule of glucose burned, anaerobic glycolysis yields two molecules of ATP, but no bonus of NADH to be converted to ATP through the ETSC. With inadequate oxygen, mitochondrial metabolism proceeds poorly, if at all.

Therefore, when glucose brain fuel is burned without adequate oxygen, it produces only 5% as much ATP energy as when glucose is burned with adequate oxygen!

Why is ATP so important? There are three main functions for ATP inside neurons:

1. Cell maintenance: Since neurons don't reproduce and must last a lifetime, they are continually expending energy to repair or replace various cell components – cell membrane segments, microtubules, mitochondria, etc.

2. Neurotransmitters: Neurons also use ATP to produce, transport, package, secrete, and reuptake neurotransmitters, such as acetylcholine and serotonin, which provide vital cell to cell communication.

3. Electrical: Huge amounts of ATP are necessary to

facilitate the frequent discharges of electrical energy from the neuron through the cell body to the transmitting end – the axon. For this electrical process to occur there must be a rapid and continuous exchange of sodium and potassium ions back and forth across the neuronal membranes.

This exchange process depends on sodium-potassium pumps, powered by sodium-potassium ATPase enzyme systems. ATPase is the enzyme needed for this process to occur. As much as 45% of a neuron's ATP may be used to power the sodium-potassium pumps.

If breathing stops, or brain blood flow is interrupted even briefly, unconsciousness rapidly occurs. As the delivery of oxygen to the brain halts, neurons rapidly shift from aerobic to anaerobic energy metabolism, with a huge drop in energy production – up to 95%! There will simply not be enough ATP energy to maintain normal neuronal electrical activity and neurotransmitter discharge – the electrochemical basis for consciousness. If aerobic metabolism ceases for too long, either irreparable damage or cell death may occur.

Neuronal activities fall behind or fail resulting in various brain dysfunctions as a result of energy shortage. This information was covered in detail to give you an idea of how complex and intricate this important aspect of brain metabolism is. If adequate supplies of glucose

> **Electrical energy in the brain requires a rapid and continuous exchange of sodium and potassium ions back and forth across the neuronal membranes. This depends on sodium-potassium pumps, powered by sodium potassium ATPase enzyme systems.**

and oxygen are not present, as a result of existing circulatory problems or disruption, the impact upon our cognitive function is very significant.

Over a lifetime, subtle, slow-developing memory loss results from brain energy losses due to cerebral arteriosclerosis, ministrokes, or brief interruptions of brain blood supply, often caused by blood vessel spasm.

In addition to memory impairment, this brain energy crisis may also cause occasional confusion or lapses in concentration, learning difficulties, etc.

At a more advanced stage the brain energy crisis may show itself as senility or senile dementia, and eventually may terminate in coma or death. The severity of dementia is directly correlated to the loss of functional brain tissue, independent of the primary neuropathology.

Memory Loss and Senility

Individuals usually do not develop memory loss or senility overnight. The deteriorative processes can begin at any age, often by the time one reaches 40 or 45. (Garcia) This deterioration is also something that does not necessarily occur in everyone. Senility is **not** a normal part of getting older. It is true that in normal people a significant number of brain cells die every year that do not regenerate. If we live long enough, there is some that occur in the normal healthy brain tissue that compensate for the slow loss of tissue.

1. The myelin sheath that covers the fibers that carry nerve impulses away from the nerve cell becomes thicker. This thickening is associated with increasing function throughout life.

2. The second compensation is that the fibers that bring impulses to the brain develop more branches, producing improved communication between all remaining cells. The better the communication between cells, the better you can perform mental and physically.

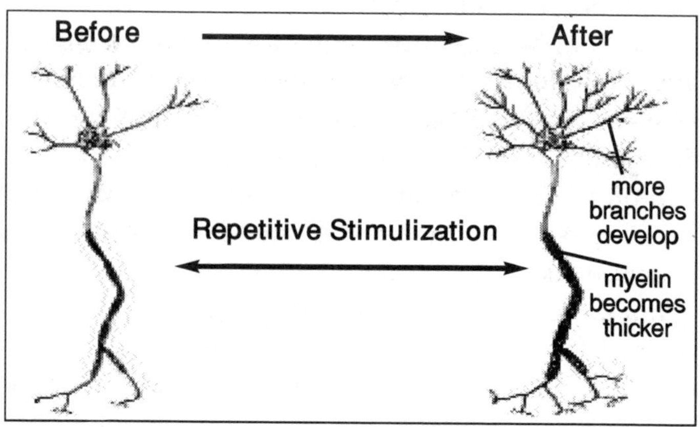

This demonstrates that senility is not natural. In fact, older individuals can actually learn easier than the young. Older individuals also reason better and can remember just as well.

If someone's brain is not working correctly, it is largely because of brain disease (such as Alzheimer's, Parkinson's, brain tumor, infection, vascular disturbances) or injury (such as from brain trauma, stroke, stress, and brain toxins such as alcohol or drugs). Nutritional factors can also play a role. Deficiencies of docosahexaenoic acid (DHA), an essential fatty acid, or B complex vitamins can also cause problems. Most of these problems can be prevented.

Symptoms of Cognitive Deterioration

Cognitive deterioration can involve the loss or decline of any of the cognitive functions such as:

- Memory
- Attention
- Orientation
- Perception
- Information fixation
- Judgement

What Causes Cognitive Deterioration?

Some of the major contributing factors to cognitive degeneration include the following:

✧ **Chronic cerebral circulatory insufficiency, etc.** This includes a variety of medical conditions which decrease the delivery of blood flow to the brain. This reduces glucose, oxygen and nutrients to the brain cells.

✧ **Various cerebral disorders** such as Alzheimer's or Parkinson's diseases.

✧ **Cerebral hemorrhage**

✧ **Stroke**

✧ **Transient ischaemic attacks** (interrupted blood flow)

✧ **Various brain toxic substances:**

-- Alcohol, opiates (morphine, heroine), cocaine, amphetamines and hallucinogens (STP, MDA, marijuana, LSD, etc.), and barbiturates.

✧ **Various prescribed psychiatric drugs** which may be very toxic to the brain causing memory loss, confusion or depression. These include:

-- Pain killers, antidepressants, sleeping pills and tranquilizers such as Valium (diazepam) and Ativan, Thoazine, Stelazine, Haldol and lithium.

✧ **Other medications** that may have an adverse effect on brain function include:

-- Antihistimines, often taken for allergies and colds

-- Corticosteriods, anti-inflammatory agents used for a variety of reasons such as asthma, arthritis, etc.

-- Heart and blood pressure medication such as digitalis, Inderal and reserpine

-- Anti-asthma medications such as aminophylline

-- Anti-gastric drugs, such as cimetidine

Combining too many different medications can also be very toxic to the brain.

Individuals with dementia attributed to Alzheimer's or to vascular disease also often have a disturbance in antioxidant balance that may predispose one to increased oxidative stress. This may be a potential therapeutic area for antioxidant supplementation. (Sinclair)

Decrease in Circulation and Cellular Efficiency Causes Many Mental Impairments

Many degenerative brain disorders are accompanied by decreased circulation and diminished cellular efficiency. While the causes of common brain disorders are diverse and complex, it stands to reason that any agent which can enhance cerebral efficiency overall would thereby enhance cognitive function. In the case of vinpocetine, this proves to be so in many cases.

Animal studies on the brain-enhancing effects of vinpocetine are voluminous. The circulatory and cognitive-enhancing effects of vinpocetine have been studied on dogs, rats, guinea pigs, and rabbits, with impressive results. While vinpocetine improves numerous physiological parameters in animals, it is the tests conducted with vinpocetine on humans that demonstrate its real value.

Lack of Stimulus

The old saying *"use it, or lose it"* certainly applies to brain functions. If we exercise our brain, it will continue to develop, evolve, etc. If we don't, we may actually suffer a loss of functioning as the years go by.

Studies show that as long as we continue to "use our brain" by exposing it to new stimuli through continuing education, doing things like crossword puzzles and playing Scrabble®, the cells in specifically the hippocampus region will continue to regenerate.

Note: Watching television is not considered brain stimulus. In fact, it may be detrimental to the brain. An interesting article was published in *Medical Hypotheses*,

"Does excessive television viewing contribute to the development of dementia?" It discussed the causes of dementia and questioned the role of excessive watching of television. The stated reasons television may contribute to the development of dementive processes included:

1. Television spectators are exposed to a mass of successive and rapid stimuli with little or no possibility of relating to the viewing matter.

2. A considerable part of television material is stress-causing, and generally there is no opportunity for a subsequent release of tension. Stress, via the glucocorticosteroids that it induces, has been shown to damage neurons in the hippocampus, a brain region involved in memory processes. Considering that many individuals have by now been watching television for several decades, not infrequently at an average rate of four or more hours daily, it is possible that cumulative, stress-derived damage may magnify the risk of a dementive process in such long-term, habitual viewers. (Aronson)

The hippocampus region, located in the back portion of the brain is highly involved in cognitive function and memory formation. As we approach advanced age, this area of the brain typically shows shrinkage ranging from 1% (in women) to 15 to 40% (more typical of men).

While the regeneration of new cells, including neurons, in the adult human brain had not yet been demonstrated before 1998, scientists in Sweden indicated through their DNA research that the human hippocampus retains its ability to generate neurons throughout life. (Eriksson)

This group of researchers also demonstrated later that environmental cues can actually enhance neurogenesis in the adult hippocampal region of laboratory rats. (Nilsson) We may be able to expect the same in humans, but we will have to wait for the research to know for sure.

Introduction to Vinpocetine:
For Enhanced Memory and Mental Function

Vinpocetine is derived from vincamine, which is an extract of the periwinkle plant (Vinca minor). Vinpocetine originates from Voacanga seed and Crioceras Longiflorus Plant, primarily used today as industrial sources for vincamine, an alkaloid used widely in geriatrics for the treatment of cerebral senility.

Vinpocetine is often used for the treatment of cerebral circulatory disorders such as memory problems, acute stroke, aphasia (loss of the power of expression), apraxia (inability to coordinate movements), motor disorders, dizziness and other cerebro-vestibular (inner-ear) problems, and headache. Vinpocetine is also used to treat acute or chronic ophthalmological diseases of various origin, with visual acuity improving in 70% of the subjects.

Vinpocetine has a very powerful stimulating effect on memory. This is the result of its effects on the brains metabolism. Vinpocetine increases the metabolism in the brain in four ways:

1. It pumps up the blood flow

2. It increases the rate at which brain cells produce ATP (which is the cell molecule that creates energy)

3. It speeds up the use of glucose in the brain

4. It speeds up the use of oxygen in the brain

The result is that the cells of the brain can better retain information, and the individual can remember more. Because of its stimulating effect on blood flow, vinpocetine has been used to treat circulatory problems in the brain and memory problems due to low circulation.

Gedeon Richter, a Hungarian company that markets vinpocetine in Europe, has funded more than a hundred studies to show it's effectiveness and safety. Many of these studies have shown the drug's powerful effect on memory improvement.

Vinpocetine facilitates cerebral metabolism by improving cerebral microcirculation (blood flow), increasing brain cell ATP production (and therefore, energy), and utilization of glucose and oxygen.

What all this means is that vinpocetine has the combined attributes of several other cognitive enhancers.

Vinpocetine is shown to compare favorably to a number of other substances known to enhance brain circulation such as vincamine, papaverine, DHT (Hydergine), xanthinol nicotinate, meclophenoxate, cinnarizine, niacin, cyclandelate, difenidol, and ifenprodil.

One of the first questions that researchers set out to answer is whether vinpocetine crosses the blood-brain barrier. A study published in the *Journal of Pharmaceutical and Biomedical Analysis* reported that chemical analysis of cerebrospinal fluid shows the presence of vinpocetine shortly after administration, proving that vinpocetine does indeed cross the blood-brain barrier.

At Iwate Medical University in Japan, patients ages 69–76 were given doses of 15 mg. vinpocetine daily for three weeks. Analysis showed that vinpocetine increased the concentration of ATP, enhanced the oxygen release of hemoglobin, and enhanced vasodilation in the brain.

To further demonstrate the physiological effects of vinpocetine, a study of patients with cerebral circulatory disorders was conducted at the Rohju Sanitarium in Osaka, Japan. Using ultrasound techniques, researchers demonstrated a significant improvement in cerebral circulation. This study, and others of a similar nature, confirmed results previously obtained with animals.

How Does Vinpocetine Work?

Cognitive functions, including, memory, are extremely complicated phenomena to study and difficult to understand. Vinpocetine has many different effects of varying importance on cognitive function. The final result of these effects is the improvement of cognitive function.

Studies performed on vinpocetine show that it works in the brain in the following four ways: it enhances vascular circulation in the brain, increases the production of ATP (the primary form of stored energy in cells) in the brain, improves the brain's utilization of oxygen and improves the brain's metabolism of glucose. By acting in these four ways, vinpocetine improves over all cerebral efficiency.

1. Improves Cerebral Metabolism

Vinpocetine improves four different and fundamental aspects of cerebral metabolism. Many studies have been performed on cerebral metabolism as it is immediate and practical to measure. But this is not the most interesting aspect of vinpocetine. It is important to note that vinpocetine is not only a cerebral vasodilator, but that its principal action consists in a beneficial action on cerebral metabolism.

2. Improves Cerebral Blood Flow

Vinpocetine selectively enhances brain circulation and oxygen utilization without significant alteration in parameters of systemic circulation. (Kiss) This is an advantage over many other substances that may increase blood flow, as they may also increase blood pressure, which in many cases would be detrimental.

Vinpocetine inhibits platelet aggregation and decreases red blood cells deformability. This allows an increased tolerance of the brain from damage from hypoxia (lack of oxygen) and ischemia (interruption of blood flow). (Kiss)

3. Increases Glucose Use in the Brain

Both experimental animal and human clinical research have shown vinpocetine restores impaired brain carbohydrate/energy metabolism. Reports indicate vinpocetine's ability to safely and effectively restore failing neuronal energy metabolism, even under hypoxic or ischaemic conditions.

In 1976 researchers reported their favorable results with vinpocetine in treating 143 patients with various cerebrovascular diseases. They proved that vinpocetine enhances both glycolytic and oxidative reactions of glucose breakdown in brain. The changes in the concentration of K [potassium] and Mg [magnesium] may be considered a sign of recovery of the energy metabolism of the nerve cells. (Vamosi)

Sodium/Potassium Channel Regulation Improves Memory

Animal studies show that increasing cerebral glucose levels enhances learning and memory. The exact mechanism for this effects is as yet uncertain. Researchers suggest that one mechanism by which glucose might act on memory and other brain functions is by regulating the potassium channel which is dependent upon adequate ATP supplies. Adequate energy (via ATP) is required for neurotransmitter release. (Stefani, Meiri)

Researchers have also shown that slowed potassium conductance results in long delays to firing during depolarization and additionally, the slow recovery from inactivation produced an increase in neuronal excitability.

These data demonstrated that slowing down the

potassium conduction can produce a form of cellular short-term memory that is independent of any changes in synaptic efficacy. (Turrigiano)

Researchers in Hungary demonstrated the effects of three vinca derivatives on sodium/potassium channels. Vinpocetine, vincamine, and vincanol blocked maximal electric shock-induced convulsions in a dose-dependent manner. The findings indicated that all three vinca derivatives are potent blockers of voltage-gated sodium channels, which is believed to contribute to their memory enhancing/cognitive benefits. (Erdo)

Researchers at the National Institutes of Health, Bethesda, MD. report that long-term memory is thought to be dependent upon by the functional remodeling of neuronal circuits. This cellular maintenance process requires adequate energy supplies. Changes in the existing synapses in networks might depend on voltage-gated potassium currents.

4. Increases Oxygen Use in the Brain

In a review on the use of vinca alkaloids in dementia, it was observed that vincamine increases mitochondrial respiratory rate, indicating that vinca alkaloids can increase the rate of ATP synthesis. The increase of ATP availability is believed to contribute to the metabolic activity of vinpocetine. (Nicholson)

Vinpocetine Affects Locus Coeruleus (LC) Neurons

Key memory-enhancing benefits from vinpocetine are also derived from its activating effect on the noradrenaline nerve cluster in the brain called the "locus coeruleus." The locus coeruleus (LC) has been implicated in processes related to regulating behaviors, learning and memory, anxiety, stress, the sleep-wake cycle, and autonomic control, as well as to contributing to the affective state. (Van Bockstaele)

Olpe and co-workers have shown that vincamine and some of its derivatives (vinpocetine) to be some of the most effective activators of locus coeruleus (LC) neurons. This small group of neurons extends its noradrenaline-secreting nerve fibers diffusely throughout the cerebral cortex (the thinking, planning, integrative brain).

Olpe notes that LC neurons decline in number with increasing age, with degeneration advancing slightly faster in men than women. The lessening number and activity of LC neurons that occurs with aging is known to play a significant role in the reduction of concentration, alertness, and information–processing speed and ability that occurs with aging.

Vinpocetine's ability to improve the cerebral cortical activating power of remaining LC neurons makes it a true "cognition enhancing" agent. (Olpe, Gaal)

Vinpocetine has demonstrated in animal studies to have the ability to significantly increase the firing rate of LC neurons. The effective dose range was in very good agreement with the dose range corresponding to the memory-enhancing effects of the compound. These results also supplied direct electrophysiological evidence that vinpocetine increases the activity of ascending noradrenergic pathways, which can be related to its cognitive-enhancing characteristics. (Gaal)

Other Possible Applications of Vinpocetine

Vinpocetine has been reported as showing promising results in the treatment of the following:

- Stroke – Vinpocetine increases the tolerance of the brain toward hypoxia and ischemia. Vinpocetine improves the properties of the blood and inhibits clotting. Studies in various laboratories have clearly demonstrated that vinpocetine offers significant and direct neuroprotection under both in vitro and in vivo conditions. (Kiss)

- Other conditions related to insufficient blood flow to the brain including:
    - Vertigo
    - Meniere's syndrome
    - Sleep disorders
    - Mood changes

- Depression

- Tinnitus or ringing in the ears

- Sensorineural hearing impairment and other causes of impaired hearing

- Menopausal symptoms – including migraine headaches

- Vision problems such as macular degeneration

- Convulsions – Vinpocetine demonstrates anticonvulsant properties. (Lakics, Molnar)

Vinpocetine Protects Brain Cells

Vinpocetine seems to have a protective effect on brain cells. Evidence shows that the neuroprotective action of vinpocetine is related to the inhibition of the operation of voltage-dependent neuronal sodium channels, indirect inhibition of some molecular cascades initiated by the rise of intracellular calcium levels, and, to a lesser extent, inhibition of adenosine reuptake.

Vinpocetine's neuroprotective effects were also demonstrated in a study examining its effects against a toxic agent, veratridine, which causes sodium and calcium levels to rise in isolated nerve terminals causing diminished neural activity. Vinpocetine reduced the increase of sodium induced by veratridine. The effect was concentration-dependent with vinpocetine completely preventing the increase of sodium. The calcium rise in response to veratridine was also prevented by vinpocetine. In addition, the calcium signal induced by depolarization was reduced by vinpocetine.

It is concluded that vinpocetine is capable of inhibiting voltage-dependent sodium and calcium channels, respectively. (Tretter)

Two separate groups of Hungarian researchers also demonstrated vinpocetine's protective effects against the same toxic agent, veratridine, in animals. Vinpocetine was highly effective in inhibiting the cell death evoked by the toxic agent. These data suggest that the blockade of voltage-gated sodium channels is a possible mechanism of action for the well-known neuroprotective and anticonvulsant properties of vinpocetine. (Lakics, Molnar)

Researchers in Russia showed that vinpocetine blocks delayed rectified potassium currents more strongly than high-threshold calcium currents. The effects of vinpocetine were dose-dependent and were independent of the test stimulus voltage. Maximum blockade of the calcium current averaged 27%. Maximum blockade of the potassium current averaged 76%. It was therefore concluded that potassium channels are more likely targets of vinpocetine than calcium channels. (Bukanova)

Vinpocetine May Help Control Seizures

Convulsions or seizures are a hyperexcitation of neurons in the brain leading to a sudden, violent involuntary series of contractions of a group of muscles. The causes are many and varied and there are many types of seizures.

Vinpocetine's ability to block voltage-gated sodium channels is believed to be a possible mechanism of action for its anticonvulsant properties. (Lakics, Molnar)

Vinpocetine and Alzheimer's

As valuable as vinpocetine may be in enhancing cerebral circulation and cognitive function among a wide range of individuals, studies are not so promising for individuals with Alzheimer's disease. In a study of 15 Alzheimer's patients at the V.A. Medical Center in San Diego, California, vinpocetine was administered in doses of 30, 45, and 60 mg. per day for one year. No improvements were noted and the conclusion of the study was that vinpocetine is ineffective in improving Alzheimer's-related cognitive deficits and does nor appear to slow the rate of decline in individuals with the disease.

Stroke

One especially exciting finding for vinpocetine is that it may play a valuable role in preventing stroke. Stroke is defined as an abnormal condition of the brain characterized by the blockage of blood flow caused by a blood clot or hemorrhage. This results in ischemia (loss of oxygenated blood) of the brain tissues normally supplied by the damaged vessels. Paralysis, speech loss, weakness, other loss of cognitive function, or death may result.

Vinpocetine increases the tolerance of the brain toward hypoxia and ischemia. Vinpocetine improves the properties of the blood and inhibits clotting. Studies in various laboratories clearly demonstrated that vinpocetine offers significant and direct neuroprotection both under in vitro and in vivo conditions. (Kiss)

In a study conducted at the Nagoya University School of Medicine in Japan, vinpocetine demonstrated the ability to enhance red blood cell deformability in the brain. The reduction of red blood cell deformability, and the subsequent rigidification of red blood cells, is a well-known contributing factor in stroke.

The effects of vinpocetine on the cerebral glucose metabolism of chronic stroke patients have been studied. The researchers' findings indicate that a single-dose vinpocetine treatment, although it does not affect significantly the regional or global metabolic rates of glucose, significantly improves the transport of glucose (both uptake and release) through the blood-brain barrier in the whole brain. (Szakall)

Vinpocetine Reduces Resistance of Cerebral Vessels

Japanese researchers investigated the effects of vinpocetine on isolated blood vessels. The results indicated that vinpocetine selectively dilates the cerebral artery, and that it may be a useful agent for the treatment of cerebrovascular diseases such as stroke.

The effect of vinpocetine on cerebral vascular resistance in patients with cerebrovascular diseases

Changes in cerebral vascular resistance were examined in patients with cerebral circulatory diseases after supplementing vinpocetine for two months. Continuous index and pulsatility index of the blood flow pattern in the internal carotid artery were used as objective parameters for changes in cerebral vascular resistance.

1. The continuous index and pulsatility index of the blood flow pattern changed significantly after administration of vinpocetine (the continuous index increased while the pulsatility index decreased).

2. An inverse correlation was noted between the rate of change of the continuous index (delta CI) and that of the pulsatility index (delta PI). (Miyazaki)

Vinpocetine has this effect on vessels as it selectively inhibits certain enzyme activity (such as phosphodiesterase) which leads to reduced resistance of cerebral vessels and increase of cerebral flow which would reduce the risk of stroke. (Kiss)

Possible value of vinpocetine in the treatment of stroke/brain damage

A four-week study conducted at Japan's Yokufukai Geriatric Hospital examined the effects of vinpocetine on patients suffering from stroke, cerebral hemorrhage, cerebral arteriosclerosis, and transient ischemic attacks. Of the 207 patients studied, 67% of patients taking 5 mg. of vinpocetine three times daily experienced slight to marked improvement, without notable side effects. Given the severity of the conditions from which the patients suffered, the improvements demonstrated by vinpocetine administration are highly encouraging.

Circulation

Good blood flow to the brain is crucial for optimal brain functioning. Vascular insufficiency is defined as inadequate peripheral blood flow caused by the narrowing of vessels by atherosclerotic plaques or clots; damaged, diseased, or weak vascular walls, or smoking.

Vascular dementia, the term for loss of mental functioning due to inadequate cerebral circulation, is preventable and reversible. The sooner that cases are detected the easier it is to avoid unnecessary deterioration through appropriate preventive therapy. (Bowler)

Vinpocetine has shown in numerous clinical trials to improve peripheral, cerebral, and central circulation. One of the additional advantages of vinpocetine's ability to improve circulation is that it does so by also decreasing blood pressure and heart rate. Vinpocetine also has a more selective vasodilative effect on the vertebral and cerebral arteries than other tested substances. (Yamada)

Karpati and Szporny conducted a study with cats. They reported that transitory and partial interference even with normal cerebral circulation caused an increase of neurochemical disturbances due to hypoxia. A deficient formation of intermediaries in the Krebs cycle was also observed, mainly due to shortage of oxygen. These and other studies refer to a selective failure of mitochondrial metabolism. Vinpocetine had favorable effects on these parameters. It seems probable that the beneficial effects of vinpocetine are most pronounced in iding vascular insufficiency problems. (Biro)

Dementia

Dementias and other severe cognitive dysfunction states pose a daunting challenge to existing medical management strategies. The sooner intervention can be done, the better the results. While, allopathic treatment options are highly limited, nutritional and botanical therapies such as vinpocetine are available which have proven degrees of efficacy and generally favorable bene-fit-to-risk profiles. (Kidd)

Dementia is often an age-related loss of mental function. The risk for confusion, memory loss, and other impairments increases with age.

Researchers have been encouraged by the positive effects seen with vinpocetine for memory enhancement in older individuals. In a double-blind study of 22 elderly patients suffering from central nervous system degenerative disorders conducted at the University of Cagliari in Italy, 87% experienced improvement in all parameters of neurological and cognitive function after 90 days, as assessed by the Clinical Global Impressions and Sandoz Clinical Assessment inventories. No significant side effects were noted.

Patients in the study were given 10 mg. of vinpocetine daily for the initial 30 days of the study, and 5 mg. three times daily for the remaining 60 days. This study demonstrates that elderly individuals suffering from age-associated cognitive impairment can indeed benefit from taking vinpocetine.

At the University of Surrey in Britain, a placebo-controlled, randomized, double-blind study examined the effects of vinpocetine on 203 patients suffering from mild to moderate psychosyndromes including primary dementia. According to two different methods of assessment, administration of vinpocetine significantly improved cognitive performance, with no notable side effects.

Improvement for Vascular-Based Cognitive Dysfunction

Vinpocetine is an excellent vasodilator and cerebral metabolic enhancer with proven benefits for vascular-based cognitive dysfunction. This is referring to problems caused by inadequate blood flow to the brain such as memory loss, learning disability, confusion, etc.

Hundreds of studies on vinpocetine have been done, often comparing its effects to other cognitive enhancers. The incidence of side effects in humans using the drug orally is usually less than 1% of a study's participants, with the unwanted effects disappearing with discontinued use.

One series of studies involved 882 patients with neurological disorders ranging from stroke to cerebral insufficiency. Significant improvements were found in 62% of the patients. In one of the studies, cerebral insufficiency patients were asked to memorize a list of 10 words. Without vinpocetine the subjects were able to memorize an average of 6 words. After a month of treatment the average went up to 10 words. Vinpocetine as the only drug that improves cerebral metabolism (glucose and oxygen metabolism, hypoxia tolerance, increased ATP concentration, and increased norepineph-

> **Significant improvements were found in 62% of the patients using vinpocetine.**
>
> **Without vinpocetine the subjects were able to memorize an average of 6 words. After a month of treatment the average went up to 10 words.**

rine and serotonin turnover), cerebral microcirculation, and selectively increases blood flow to the brain (improving blood flow to the impaired area without lowering blood flow to other parts of the body).

The *Journal of the American Geriatric Society* reported the results of a double-blind trial in which 42 patients with chronic vascular senile cerebral dysfunction were given 10 mg. of vinpocetine three times daily for 40 days, then 5 mg. three times daily for 60 days. Patients were tested using the Clinical Global Impression Scale, the Sandoz Clinical Assessment Geriatric Scale and the MiniMental Status Questionnaire. Significant improvements were observed across the board, without any significant side effects.

Oxygen affinity of hemoglobin, red blood cell 2, 3-diphosphoglycerate (DPG) and ATP concentrations were compared before and after oral administration of vinpocetine,15 mg./day, for three weeks in eight patients with vascular dementia of the Biswanger type (characterized by diffuse myelin pallor and multiple lacunes in the cerebral white matter).

After vinpocetine administration, the oxygen affinity of hemoglobin significantly increased (26.5 to 27.6 mmHg), red blood cell ATP concentrations significantly increased (approximately 846 to 1,158 mumol/l RBC), while DPG concentrations were unaltered (4.46 to 4.59 mmol/l RBC). There was a significant positive correlation between the increase of oxygen affinity of hemoglobin and the increase of red blood cell ATP concentrations.

The effect of vinpocetine of enhancing oxygen release of hemoglobin may offer an additional benefit to its primary vasodilating action in the treatment of vascular dementia of the Binswanger type due to chronic ischemia. (Tohgi)

Cognitive Enhancement

While many studies focus on the effects of vinpocetine for patients suffering from various degenerative conditions, researchers have also inquired into the effects of this agent in healthy individuals. In a German study 40 healthy volunteers were given 40 mg. of vinpocetine daily for two days. This brief course resulted in a significant improvement in memory as assessed by the Sternberg Memory Scanning Test. This study suggests that in normal, healthy people, vinpocetine can enhance memory, and can do so quickly.

Clinical Trials on Young and Healthy Volunteers

In a series of three studies at the University of Leeds, the team of Dr. Hindmarch performed three clinical trials with young and healthy volunteers (aged 25-40). They used the Sternberg Memory Test to base their evaluation.

The studies showed a memory improvement in volunteers and this improvement was related to the dose of vinpocetine used. It is important to note that these trials were double blind crossed, which are the strictest clinical trials. Neither the doctors nor the patients knew if they were taking the product or placebo. The significant difference clearly shows the efficacy of vinpocetine on young and healthy individuals.

Clinical Trials with the Elderly

Over more than 100 clinical trials have been performed with vinpocetine, and some of them, have studied its specific action on memory, as well as its general action of vinpocetine in the brain. The majority of these studies were performed with elderly patients, on a total of over 20,000 patients. These studies were performed in several

Memory improvement was seen in 75–85% of geriatric patients with vinpocetine.

countries, such as Japan, Russia, (former USSR), United Kingdom, Germany, Italy, Portugal, etc. For example, there is a series of trials performed by three different teams in Italy and published in well known international scientific publications, such as the *Journal of American Geriatric Society*. In these three studies involving approximately 120 patients, an improvement of memory was observed in 75% to 86% of these patients following the Sandoz Clinical Assessment Geriatric Scale criteria.

Short-Term Memory Improvement

Short-term memory involves temporary changes in the function of the neurons. When stimulated once, the neurons in the areas of the brain involving sensation and motor functions demonstrate an increased sensitivity to neurotransmission.

In one double-blind crossover study, normal, healthy volunteers showed incredible short-term memory improvement one hour after taking 40 mg. of vinpocetine. The volunteers took a computer-administered short-term memory test. The volunteers (all women between the ages of 25 and 40) were shown one to three digits on a computer screen, then a moment later were shown a long string of digits. The volunteers then indicated whether any of the first digits appeared in the second long string. The time the volunteer took to remember was then assessed. On a placebo the women took an average of 700 milliseconds to respond when the first set contained 3 digits. With vinpocetine they averaged under 450 milliseconds! (Subhan).

The effects of pre-treatment with vinpocetine 40 mg. on induced impairment of memory, were studied in eight normal volunteers. This treatment with vinpocetine was also associated with improvements in short-term memory processes. (Bhatti)

Enhancement of Learning and Recall

Memory and learning are not the same. Learning is actually the first process of memory formation, the second step recall - retrieving the learned information.

Several passive avoidance response tests have been conducted in rats with Vinpocetine, and evaluated its ability to prevent scopolamine-induced and hypoxia-induced impairment of passive-avoidance retention (24 hour) in rats. The data support the view that vinpocetine has a cognitive activating ability as defined in models of both scopolamine-induced and hypoxia-induced memory impairment in rats. (DeNoble, Okuyama)

In another study, vinpocetine, vincamine, apovincaminic acid, vinconate, aniracetam, Hydergine, and pemoline were evaluated for their ability to enhance retrieval of a step-through passive-avoidance response in rats. The percentage of rats performing the avoidance response was found to decrease as a function of the number of days between training and retention testing (Day 1, 100%; Day 2, 65%; Day 3, 23%; Days 4 and 5, 0%).

Vinpocetine given 60 minutes prior to testing for retention significantly increased the number of rats performing the passive avoidance response. Retrieval enhancement was dose-related.

In contrast, apovincaminic acid, vincamine, vinconate, aniracetam, Hydergine, and pemoline were not effective. These data support that vinpocetine has recall or retrieval of information activating abilities as defined in an animal model. (DeNoble)

Vinpocetine can be helpful improving the formation of new memories when used during the process of learning. New studies are in progress.

Vinpocetine for Lack of Attention and Concentration

There is no evidence of specific scientific tests on the capacity of attention or concentration with vinpocetine. However, different tests of geriatric assessment do include parameters to measure them and these capacities have been proven to be improved with vinpocetine using tests other than the above. As attention and concentration are cognitive functions, vinpocetine can be recommended when the deterioration of these capacities is observed.

What vinpocetine users say:

This is the first product in my recollection that actually makes me "smart". I am now able to tackle tasks that used to require more time or planning. I can now carry on a more intelligent conversation with people in general. I believe I have found the pill that is transforming my life for the better. I only wish I had taken this 20 years ago because I believe my life would be very different today. W. S.

Because I have ADD, I am interested in "brain nutrients." From what I originally read about vinpocetine and combined with what I know of the neurochemical aspects of ADD showed me it may be helpful. ADD brains have lower glucose levels for one, and vinpocetine raises glucose. I was right. Vinpocetine has had a noticeable effect on my cognitive functioning, especially regarding my ADD. I think better and remember more, and I don't "trip" over my ADD like before. It's hard to explain, but suffice it to say that the vinpocetine is working. I wonder if there's any formal research being done regarding this supplement and ADD. I take 10 milligrams per day. Thanks, V.C.

Vinpocetine Increases Neurotransmitters

Vinpocetine has a multiple of actions resulting in overall cognitive enhancement. One of the additional causes of vinpocetine's many and varied effects are due to its effects on several important neurotransmitters. These are specialized brain chemicals involved in the transfer of information between neurons.

While memory is an extremely complex phenomenon, neuronal transmission is even more complex. There are more than 100 different identified neurotransmitters, and until now we still do not know which are the functions of each nor why there are so many.

Depressed levels of certain neurotransmitters are associated with psychiatric disorders, such as serotonin and depression, and dopamine and Parkinson's. But these associations are not exclusive.

This is one reason it is so difficult to explain how vinpocetine works. Vinpocetine at a dosage of just 5 mg. effects neurotransmission. Also, the empirical formula of Vinpocetine is very similar to that of neurotransmitters.

Neurotransmitters are responsible for the transmission between neurons, indicating that they are necessary for all cognitive functions. Vinpocetine increases the levels of various neurotransmitters which gives us a basis of its ways of action. Vinpocetine seems to act on neuronal transmission.

1. Vinpocetine increases levels of noradrenaline, the neurotransmitter found principally in neurons of the locus coeruleus (LC) area of the brain. This area is known to be involved in thinking, planning, learning, etc. (Paulo)

2. Vinpocetine increases levels of dopamine, (Kiss) the neurotransmitter found in various neuronal areas such as the nigrostriatal, mesolimbic, and meso-cortical. Dopamine generally facilitates informational transfer within limbic and cortical networks to promote reward-seeking behavior. Specifically, dopamine activity in prefrontal cortex modulates the ability for nonhuman primates and humans to perform spatial working memory tasks. (Luciana)

Disorders at this level have been related to schizophrenia. Low levels of dopamine are associated with Parkinson's disease. Dopamine is the precursor to another neurotransmitter, norepinephrine.

3. Vinpocetine increases levels of acetylcholine, a neurotransmitter found in large amounts in many areas of the central nervous system, principally in the basal ganglions and cerebral cortex. It is associated with memory and memory loss. (Milusheva, Matsukawa)

Japanese researchers demonstrated the importance of serotonin and acetylcholine to memory acquisition. Their data suggested that synapses in the hippocampus that are normally maintained by serotonin and acetylcholine are crucial for normal acquisition of spatial memory. The number of synapses maintained by neurotransmitters may be a basic mechanism for neurobehavioral plasticity. (Matsukawa)

4. Vinpocetine increases levels of serotonin, the neurotransmitter commonly associated with mood regulation and sleep. Low levels have been associated with depression, sleep disorders, addiction disorders, appetite disorders, etc. (Shibuya)

Serotonin Deficiencies

Serotonin is a brain chemical recognized to regulate sleep, pain, appetite, and emotions. (Jacobs) Levels of serotonin do decline with age, according to research performed at the University of Pittsburgh Medical Center, which demonstrated a 55% decrease in serotonin receptors.

Increasing levels of serotonin, by supplementing precursors such as tryptophan and 5-hydroxytryptophan (5-HTP) have shown to improve memory, learning and executive functioning. Animal studies showed that young animals also benefited from small doses of 5-HTP, although not as much as the aging animals benefited. (Matsukawa)

Since neurotransmission of serotonin and acetylcholine is simultaneously activated during the spatial memory task, researchers suggest that these neurotransmitter systems regulate behavioral and cognitive functions. (Stancampiano)

Vinpocetine increases the level of serotonin in the brain. Researchers in France demonstrated in 1999 that low levels of serotonin diminished cellular proliferation in certain areas of the hippocampus (the subventricular zone and the subgranular zones) in adult rats. Lack of serotonin has also been associated with cognitive disorders, such as depression, schizophrenia, and Alzheimer's disease. The French study demonstrated that both inhibition of serotonin synthesis and selective lesions of serotonin neurons are associated with decreases in the number of newly generated cells in these two hippocampal zones.

A few studies have suggested that serotonin may play a role in neuronal regeneration by maintaining the synaptic connections in the cortex and hippocampus, but no information is actually available concerning the influence of serotonin on adult brain cell formation. Further work may confirm that new neurons can be produced in the adult human brain. (Brezun)

This indicates that substances known to enhance serotonin levels may be of benefit to cognitive disorders. This is, of course, the reason for many SSRI (Selective Serotonin Reuptake Inhibitor) drugs such as Paxil and Prozac commonly prescribed for depression, anxiety, addiction disorders, etc.

There are no studies to my knowledge examining the effects of Vinpocetine on these specific disorders, but in theory, as it increases serotonin in the brain, it should be helpful.

Depression

In addition to prominent memory loss, depression may be a symptom of cerebral vascular insufficiency or vascular dementia. Serotonin neuron and neurotransmitter loss in normal aging and neuropsychiatric diseases is also commonly known to contribute to the development of major depression. (Meltzer)

Recent research has identified that various abnormalities in serotonergic function are involved in the pathogenesis of depression and anxiety, and has facilitated the development of new pharmacological agents with great therapeutic potential, for example the selective serotonin reuptake inhibitors (SSRIs). These agents appear to be effective in the treatment of many depression and anxiety states and may have greater efficacy than other agents in the treatment of certain affective disorders. (Baldwin)

While no published studies have been conducted specifically on the effects of vinpocetine and depression or anxiety, because vinpocetine increases levels of serotonin in the brain, one could safely assume that depression may be relieved as a result.

Headaches

The relationship between serotonin and headaches, particularly migraine headaches is a relatively new concept and is still under investigation to fully understand.

A role for serotonin in migraine has been supported by changes in circulating levels of serotonin and its metabolites during the phases of a migraine attack, along with the ability of serotonin-releasing agents to induce migraine-like symptoms. The development of serotonin receptor agonists with efficacy in the clinic for the alleviation of migraine pain further implicates serotonin as a key molecule in migraine. (Johnson)

Many anti-migraine drugs interact with serotonin and its receptors. (Silberstein)

Italian researchers suggest that serotonin availability is reduced in migraine headaches caused by PMS, possibly due to an increased catabolism and/or to a reduced synthesis, and hence predisposes patients to migraine attacks. (Fioroni)

The data suggest that agents such as vinpocetine, which increase serotonin levels, may also be beneficial in preventing or treating individuals with migraine headaches.

Sleep Disorders

Serotonin levels are also widely known to regulate sleep. Ever wonder why a glass of warm milk before bedtime is supposed to help you sleep better? Milk is high in the amino acid tryptophan, which is a precursor to serotonin.

Sleep disorders (such as chronic drowsiness) can also result from insufficient blood flow to the brain. (Tagawa) Patients with cerebrovascular insufficiency experience disturbances in the regulation of both phases of nocturnal sleep. (Gafurov) Therefore, vinpocetine may also be of assistance for these individuals as well as it increases blood flow to the brain.

Again, studies have not been conducted in this area with vinpocetine, but it may be helpful for sleep disorders and other disorders related to abnormal serotonin levels. This also includes addiction disorders (alcoholism, drug addiction, etc.), and eating disorders such as anorexia and bulimia.

There are some reports of taking vinpocetine at night causing sleeplessness. This is likely due to the increase in nuerotransmitter activity. If this occurs, I simply suggest that the supplement be taken in the morning, which does not interfere with sleep,

Alcoholism and Memory Loss

Researchers have recently revealed that one of the causes of memory loss (and also depression) may be due to changes in noradrenergic neurotransmission due to fewer noradrenergic neurons in the locus coeruleus (LC).

Alcoholics were found to have 23% fewer LC neurons compared to non-drinking controls and 46% lower density of neurons. (Arango) This suggests that vinpocetine may be of assistance to the recovering alcoholic in helping to restore noradrenergic levels in the locus coeruleus. More research is needed in this area.

Other Benefits of Vinpocetine

The potential benefits of vinpocetine are very large. Many areas of potential benefit have not yet been studied. Any health problem associated with diminished cerebral circulation could potentially benefit. For example, preliminary research shows vinpocetine may be helpful for hair loss associated with inadequate cerebral blood flow. Following are some of the additional potential benefits of vinpocetine.

Cardiovascular Health

While vinpocetine increases the cerebral fraction of cardiac output, there is no marked effect on systemic circulation and blood pressure. Total vascular resistance decreases very slightly with vinpocetine. Since vinpocetine therefore actually reduces the effort of the heart, its effects may be assumed to be favorable in cerebral alterations associated with heart disease and hypertension. (Solti)

Chinese researchers studying the effects of vinpocetine found that the sodium current in cardiomyocytes was blocked reversibly by vinpocetine. In a concentration-dependent and voltage-dependent manner, the sodium current was blocked 13%-75%. When the membrane potential depolarized, the inhibitory effect of vinpocetine on the sodium current was as high as 57%. (Wei)

Hair Loss

Due to the improvement of peripheral microcirculation in microvessels of the head, some people taking vinpocetine orally, have reported are more vigorous hair condition, stating they no longer feel strong hair loss.

The most common ingredient used against hair loss is Mynoxidil, which is a strong peripheral vasodilator with adverse side effects. The mechanism of action of Vinpocetine is the same but with the advantage of no side effects. (Covex)

Studies are being performed with hydroalcoholic solutions of vinpocetine, used as hair lotions for the hair skin. (Covex) No bibliographic references have been found.

Stomach Ulcers

Vinpocetine may help ward off stomach ulcers. The effectiveness of vinpocetine to prevent gastric mucosal damage induced by several agents and its antisecretory effect was studied in rats. Vinpocetine proved to inhibit the development of gastric lesions induced by 96% ethanol in a dose-dependent way. The highest protective activity was observed when vinpocetine was given 30 minutes before ethanol, and its effect was still significant when administered 120 minutes before ethanol exposure.

The also study suggested the involvement of a prostaglandin-mediated mechanism against acetic acid-induced damage. Histamine-stimulated gastric acid secretion was partially inhibited by vinpocetine. (Nosalova)

Kidney Stones

Japanese researchers at the Wakayama Medical College showed that vinpocetine supplementation is able to remove tumoral calcinosis in kidney dialysis patients with renal (kidney) failure.

As other studies have shown that vinpocetine can effectively scavenge undesirable minerals and/or metals in the soft tissues of rabbits with artificially induced arteriosclerosis, researchers suspected that it may be of benefit to remove undesirable mineral deposits elsewhere in the body as well. In the Japanese study, after vinpocetine administration of 15 mg./day for 3-12 months, kidney dialysis patients with X-ray evidence of kidney stones (tumoral calcinosis) experienced complete elimination of calcinosis in all eight cases. Blood levels of alkaline phosphatase and bone osteocalcin tended to decrease after treatment with vinpocetine. Vinpocetine had this remarkable effect without any side-effects during treatment. (Miyata)

Tinnitus and Other Hearing Problems

Hearing dysfunction such as tinnitus (ringing in the ears) and progressive sensorineural hearing loss (PSNHL) are commonly caused by cerebral vascular factors. The increase of blood viscosity and/or increase of rigidity of the red blood cells has been reported by several authors. (Ravecca)

Tinnitus is one of the problems for which vinpocetine has been most studied and results are very promising. (Taiji, Konopke, Ordogh, Ribari, Matsnev)

Vascular problems of the inner ear such as tinnitus can benefit from vinpocetine as it has been used for the hearing loss of senile or toxic origin and laberinthic vertigos (dizziness), which are all inner ear disorders of vascular origin.

What vinpocetine users say:

Five days after I began taking Intelectol (brand of vinpocetine), I noticed that the intensity of sound associated with my tinnitis had decreased significantly. Now after taking Intelectol for two months, the constant background noise which had become part of my life is usually absent in my left ear, and is about half as loud as before Intelectol in my right ear. In addition, I seem to be thinking more clearly and am less prone to the blues. I highly recommend Intelectol to those suffering from Tinnitis and to anyone who wants the benefits of a clear head. R.G.

I am currently taking this (vinpocetine) for tinnitus and it seems to be working very well. I have been on it now for 3 weeks and the level of ringing continues to decrease. Thank you! L. B.

I have been using Vinpocetine for my tinnitus for two weeks. I am amazed with how well it works. I have been told that there is nothing that helps Tinnitus and that I have to live with it. Why is vinpocetine not prescribed for this? I have found that I get relief for about four hours. 10 mg. will provide relief in about 15 minutes.

Vision Problems

In ophthalmology vinpocetine has been used for blood flow problems of the choroid and retina, such as macular degeneration; certain problems related to glaucoma; and other vision disorders of vascular origin.

In a study with 100 patients suffering from poor blood circulation to the eye, researchers noted vinpocetine's inhibition of platelet aggregation (clotting). The microvessels that feed neurons in the brain and retina are smaller in diameter than a single red blood cell and are easily "clogged" by clumps of platelets, impairing microcirculation. This provides another mechanism of action for vinpocetine's ability to enhance cerebral blood flow-inhibition of unnecessary platelet aggregation, which may be triggered by a high fat diet, magnesium deficiency, and stress hormones, among other factors. (Kaham)

Vinpocetine Supplementation

Vinpocetine, as a natural herbal extract, has no drug interactions, no toxicity, and is generally very safe. Adverse effects from vinpocetine supplementation are rare but include hypotension, dry mouth, weakness, and tachycardia (rapid heart beat). Although vinpocetine and vincamine have many similar effects, vinpocetine has more benefits and fewer adverse effects than vincamine.

Not one single case of intoxication during 30 years of marketing has been documented with vinpocetine. After 30 years of marketing, hundreds of thousands of people have taken vinpocetine, and more than 500 million tablets have been sold, there is no evidence of any single case of oral intoxication from vinpocetine. (Covex) This can not be stated for other products such as aspirin or antibiotics.

Bioavailability increased when taken with food

A German study examined the bioavailability of vinpocetine with two groups of volunteers, one of which ate food prior to ingesting vinpocetine, and one group which did not. Results showed that bioavailability of vinpocetine was improved 60-100% by taking it with food.

Vinpocetine and apovincaminic acid are absorbed from the gastrointestinal tract–apovincaminic acid mainly from the stomach, while vinpocetine is absorbed from the small intestine. (Pudleiner)

Safety/Side Effects

Side effects are only experienced by a small number of people. Most of them are mild and disappear after the drug has been taken for awhile. Side effects are much more common with the injectable form of the drug. A brief drop in blood pressure or faster heart rate may occur in some people. So far vinpocetine has not been found to interact with other drugs, so it can be taken in combination with other medicines. A year-long toxicity study, demonstrated no ill effects. Studies carried out to determine whether vinpocetine could cause cancer revealed that it was completely safe. No change in male or female fertility was seen. No teratogenic (ability to cause defects in the unborn child) effects were seen. Vinpocetine cannot cause mutation of or cause damage to normal cells.

A major Japanese study by Otomo and colleagues with 207 patients suffering various cerebral disorders found only a 2% incidence of mild adverse side effects: anorexia in two patients, hives and stomach pain in one patient and hot flashes in another patient. No significant adverse laboratory findings occurred in the 207 vinpocetine patients (Otomo).

Animal safety tests have found that the oral lethal dosage for Vinpocetine to be approximately 534 mg./kg. of body weight for mice, 503 mg./kg. of body weight for rats. If we could relate this amount to humans, this would equate to approximately 35,000 mg. for a 150-pound human. The usual therapeutic dose for Vinpocetine for humans is 15-30 mg. per day.

Because of side effects occurring at very high doses when used with pregnant rats (uterine bleeding in some), caution is suggested for using vinpocetine in pregnant women, or those trying or expecting to get pregnant. (Cholnoky and Domok)

Overall, vinpocetine side effects reported in the literature are rare, usually minor, frequently disappear with prolonged use, and rarely require discontinuance of the product. The main (rarely occurring) reported side effects are stomach/GI upset; dry mouth, rapid heart beat, low blood pressure, and rash/hives.

Dosage

Vinpocetine is not a drug and is not a stimulant so it does not have an immediate effect after taking. It works gradually in time and its effects can be noticed after three or four weeks of intake.

The general dosage for vinpocetine is 10-40 mg. per day. Vinpocetine is normally taken orally, 5-10 mg. two or three times daily.

Some people report feeling "over-stimulated" from higher, more frequent dosing, and report as little as 2.5 mg. once or twice daily to be useful but not over-stimulating. Mild and transient nausea, though rare, is more likely to occur when vinpocetine is taken on an empty stomach.

Sublingually, results with vinpocetine may be seen at a lower dose (2.5 mg.) use, with quicker and sometimes more noticeable effect.

While some individuals need to supplement vinpocetine for weeks or months before seeing major improvement in medical situations, the cognitive enhancement benefits may be noticeable from even a single dose, or within the first several days of use.

Improvements in cerebral disorders and in hearing and vision problems may last only as long as the product continues to be taken.

Because Vinpocetine enhances cerebral blood flow, it may potentate other brain, "cerebral-activating" products taken simultaneously, thus allowing or requiring them to be taken at a lower dosage.

Some researchers have stated that it may take about a year of daily use to achieve maximum effect.

What vinpocetine users say:

I have found that taking 10 mg. 3 times/day of vinpocetine is too much! Instead, 5 mg. 3 times/day seems to give pretty good result. So, more does not mean better. I have also learned that I must take it either during or after meals, but not before otherwise I become tired. Perhaps the pill is quite strong so I need to accompany it with food. In short, I am VERY happy to have taken this product because I have tried many others before for memory and cognitive function but they just don't work as well!

Who Can Benefit from Vinpocetine?

1. The most obvious to benefit from vinpocetine supplementation are the elderly, as they have the highest degree of cognitive deterioration.

2. Anyone over age 40 can benefit from a memory boost as losses may noted at any time. Cerebral arteriosclerosis is less well known to the public than heart disease, but it is just as common, and develops gradually over a lifetime. By the time serious symptoms develop, as in heart disease, the blood vessel occlusion is usually well advanced. Vinpocetine can minimize the structural, functional damage to brain neurons that may accompany gradually developing cerebral arteriosclerosis.

3. Baby boomers may also be starting to suffer from symptoms of memory loss. Many health concerned individuals will also be interested in something to enhance their memory capacity.

4. Young people, such as students at exam time, may want to enhance their memory by using vinpocetine.

5. Anyone wishing to use a generally very safe product with low side effects to enhance brain metabolism, vigilance, and cognition will want to benefit from vinpocetine.

6. Anyone who has noticed a decrease in memory, alertness, concentration, learning speed ability, neuromuscular coordination and reaction time, vision, hearing, or who suffers from tinnitus will benefit from using vinpocetine.

7. Anyone who suffers from, or is known to be at risk for, various cerebral disorders, cerebral hemorrhage, stroke, senile dementia, transient ischaemic attacks, chronic cerebral circulatory insufficiency, etc.

Summary

Vinpocetine may not be a panacea, but it clearly demonstrates in many cases its value in enhancing brain function and cognitive ability. As we strive to retard the aging process and fight the deterioration of the brain and mind, vinpocetine, with exciting and credible science to back it up, stands to be one of the valuable agents we use for wellness into our advanced years.

Vinpocetine:

1. Is effective when taken orally.

2. Is at low risk for side effects especially when taken with food.

3. Selectively improves the blood and oxygen supply to the brain.

4. Increases the tolerance of the brain to lack of oxygen by vasodilation.

5. Enhances use of glucose by brain cells.

6. Increases ATP (energy) levels in the brain.

7. Stops or prevents blood from becoming sticky.

8. Increases levels of serotonin and other neurotransmitters.

9. Is nontoxic even in doses several times higher than those used normally. Vinpocetine is 50 times less toxic than a cup of coffee at recommended doses.

Bibliography

Arango V; Underwood MD; Mann JJ; Fewer pigmented neurons in the locus coeruleus of uncomplicated alcoholics. Brain Res 1994 Jul 4;650(1):1-8.

Aronson M Does excessive television viewing contribute to the development of dementia? Department of Cell Biology and Histology, Sackler School of Medicine, Tel-Aviv University, Israel. Medical Hypotheses 1993 Nov;41(5):465-6.

Baldwin D; Rudge S; The role of serotonin in depression and anxiety.Ealing Mental Health Unit, Southall, Middlesex, UK. Int Clin Psychopharmacol 1995 Jan;9 Suppl 4:41-5

Bhatti JZ; Hindmarch I; Vinpocetine effects on cognitive impairments produced by flunitrazepam. Human Psychopharmacology Research Unit, University of Leeds, U.K. Int Clin Psychopharmacol 1987 Oct;2(4):325-31.

Biro, K. et al; "Protective activity of Ethyl Apovincaminate on ischemic anoxia of the brain" AF(DR) 1976, 28, 1918-20.

Bowler J; Hachinski V.; Vascular cognitive impairment: a new approach to vascular dementia. University of Western Ontario, London, Canada. Baillieres Clin Neurol 1995 Aug;4(2):357-76.

Brezun J; Daszuta A; Depletion in serotonin decreases neurogenesis in the dentate gyrus and the subventricular zone of adult rats. Laboratory of Cellular and Functional Neurobiology, CNRS, UPR 9013, Marseille, France. Neuroscience 1999;89(4):999-1002.

Bukanova Y; Solntseva E; Nootropic agent vinpocetine blocks delayed rectified potassium currents more strongly than high-threshold calcium currents. Science Research Institute of the Brain, Russian Academy, Medical Sciences, Moscow. Neurosci Behav Physiol 1998 Mar-Apr;28(2):116-20.

Bukanova I; Solntseva E; [The nootropic agent vinpocetine blocks the delayed rectifier potassium channel more strongly than the high-conductance calcium channel] Zh Vyssh Nerv Deiat Im I P Pavlova 1996 Sep-Oct;46(5):911-6.

Cameron H; McKay R; Stem cells and neurogenesis in the adult brain. Laboratory of Molecular Biology, National Institutes of Health, Bethesda, Maryland Curr Opin Neurobiol 1998 Oct;8(5):677-80.

Covex, Madrid, Spain, personal conversation 11/16/99.

DeNoble V; Vinpocetine enhances retrieval of a step-through passive avoidance response in rats. Biochem Behav 1987 Jan;26(1):183-6.

DeNoble VJ; Repetti SJ; Gelpke LW; Wood LM; Keim KL; Vinpocetine: nootropic effects on scopolamine-induced and hypoxia- induced retrieval deficits of a step-through passive avoidance response in rats. Pharmacol Biochem Behav 1986 Apr;24(4):1123-8.

Eriksson PS; Perfilieva E; Bjork-Eriksson T; Alborn AM; Nordborg C; Peterson DA; Neurogenesis in the adult human hippocampus Department of Clinical Neuroscience, Institute of Neurology, Sahlgrenska University Hospital, Goteborg, Sweden. Nat Medical 1998 Nov;4(11):1313-7.

Erdo SA; Molnar P; Lakics V; Bence JZ; Tomoskozi Z; Vincamine and vincanol are potent blockers of voltage-gated Na+ channels. Laboratory of CNS Pharmacology, Chinoin Co., Budapest, Hungary. Eur J Pharmacol 1996 Oct 24;314(1-2):69-73.

Fioroni L; Andrea GD; Alecci M; Cananzi A; Facchinetti F; Platelet serotonin pathway in menstrual migraine. Department of Obstetrics and Gynaecology, University of Modena, Italy. Cephalalgia 1996 Oct;16(6):427-30.

Gaal L; Molnar P; Effect of vinpocetine on noradrenergic neurons in rat locus coeruleus. Department of Biochemistry, Chemical Works of Gedeon Richter Ltd.,Budapest, Hungary. Eur J Pharmacol 1990 Oct 23;187(3):537-9.

Gafurov BG; Busakov BS; Status of the nonspecific systems of the brain in initial manifestations of insufficiency of cerebral blood supply and circulatory encephalopathy. Zh Nevropatol Psikhiatr Im S S Korsakova. 1992;92(1):38-40.

Garcia, L., Nebreda, 0., Perlado, F.; Mental Illness in the Elderly, 1994, 9.

Taiii, H., Kanzaki, J.; "Clinical Study of Vinpocetine in the treatment of vertigo.", JPN Pharmacol Ter, 1986; 14: 577.

Jacobs BL; Fornal CA; Activity of serotonergic neurons in behaving animals. Department of Psychology, Princeton University, NJ. Neuropsychopharmacology 1999 Aug;21(2 Suppl):9S-15S.

Johnson KW; Phebus LA; Cohen ML; Serotonin in migraine: theories, animal models and emerging therapies. Lilly Research Laboratories, Eli Lilly and Company, Lilly Corporate Center, Indianapolis, IN Prog Drug Res 1998;51:219-44.

Kaham, A., OlahM., Use of Ethyl Apovincaminate in ophthalmological therapy" AF(DR) 1976; 28, 1969-72.

Kidd PM; A review of nutrients and botanicals in the integrative management of cognitive dysfunction Contributing Editor, Alternative Medicine Review.

Correspondence address:47 Elm St., El Cerrito, CA 94530, USA. Altern Medical Rev 1999 Jun;4(3):144-61.

Kiss B; Karpati E; [Mechanism of action of vinpocetine] Vinpocetine hatasai, hatasmechanizmusa. Richter Gedeon Vegyeszeti Gyar Rt., Farmakologiai Kutato Kozpont, Budapest.Acta Pharm Hung 1996 Sep;66(5):213-24.

Kiss, B., Szporny, L. et al. On the possible role of central monominergic systems in the central nervous systems actions of vinpocetine. Drug Dev. Res., (1988) 14, 263-279.

Konopke W, Zalewski P, et Al., "Treatment results of acoustic trauma", Otolaryngol Pol. 1997; 51: 281-4.

Lakics V; Sebestyen MG; Erdo SL;Vinpocetine is a highly potent neuroprotectant against veratridine- induced cell death in primary cultures of rat cerebral cortex. CNS Pharmacology Laboratory, Chinoin Co. Ltd., Budapest, Hungary. Neurosci Lett 1995 Feb 9;185(2):127-30.

Lafosse JM; Reed BR; et al Fluency and memory differences between ischemic vascular dementia and Alzheimer's disease. Alzheimer's Disease Center, University of Ca, School of Medicine, Davis, Neuropsychology 1997 Oct;11(4):514-22.

Luciana M; Collins PF; Opposing roles for dopamine and serotonin in the modulation of human spatial working memory functions. D of Psychology, U of Oregon, Eugene, Cereb Cortex 1998 Apr-May; 8(3):218-26.

Mark, V. Brain Power, Houghton Mifflin Company, Boston, MA, 1989.

Matsukawa M; Ogawa M; Nakadate K; Maeshima T; Ichitani Y; Kawai N; Serotonin and acetylcholine are crucial to maintain hippocampal synapses and memory acquisition in rats. Institute of Basic Medical Sciences, University of Tsukuba, Ibaraki, Japan. Neurosci Lett 1997 Jul 11;230(1):13-6

Matsnev, E., Bodo, D., "Experimental Assessment of Selected Antimotion Drugs". Aviation, Space and Enviromental Medicine. 1984, 55.4:281-6.

Meiri N; Ghelardini C; Tesco G; Galeotti N; Dahl D;et al; Reversible antisense inhibition of Shaker-like Kv1.1 potassium channel expression impairs associative memory in mouse and rat. National Institutes of Health, Bethesda, MD. Proc Natl Acad Sci U S A 1997 Apr 29;94(9):4430-4.

Meltzer CC; Smith G; DeKosky ST; Pollock BG;et al; Serotonin in aging, late-life depression, and Alzheimer's disease: the emerging role of functional imaging. Alzheimer's Disease Research Center, University of Pittsburgh Medical Center, PA Neuropsychopharmacology 1998 Jun;18(6):407-30.

Milusheva, E., Sperlagh, B., Kiss, B., Szporny, L. et al. Inhibitory effect of hypoxic condition on acetylcholine release is partly due to the effect of adenosine released from the tissue. Brain Res. Bull., (1990), 24, 369-373.

Miyazaki M; The effect of a cerebral vasodilator, vinpocetine, on cerebral vascular resistance evaluated by the Doppler ultrasonic technique in patients with cerebrovascular diseases. Angiology 1995 Jan;46(1): 53-8.

Miyata N; Yamaura H; Tanaka M; Muramatsu M; Tsuchida K; et al; Effects of VA-045, a novel apovincaminic acid derivative, on isolated blood vessels: cerebroarterial selectivity. Research Center, Taisho Pharmaceutical Co., Ltd., Saitama, Japan. Life Science.

Moldvai I; Temesvari-Major E; Szantay C Jr; Toth G; Karpati E; Szantay C; Synthesis of vinca alkaloids and related compounds. Part 84. Sulfonamide derivatives of some vinca alkaloids with cardiovascular activity. 1997 Jun;330(6):190-8.

Molnar P; Erdo SL; Vinpocetine is as potent as phenytoin to block voltage-gated Na+ channels in rat cortical neurons. CNS Pharmacology Laboratory, Chinoin Co. Ltd., Budapest, Hungary. Eur J Pharmacol 1995 Feb 6;273(3):303-6.

Nicholson, C. Pharmacology of nootropics and metabolically active compounds in relation to their use in dementia. Psychopharm, 1985, 101,147-59.

Nilsson M; Perfilieva E; Johansson U; Orwar O; Eriksson P; Enriched environment increases neurogenesis in the adult rat dentate gyrus and improves spatial memory. Institute of Clinical Neuroscience, Sahlgrenska University Hospital, Goteborg University, Sweden. J Neurobiol 1999 Jun 15;39(4):569-78.

Nosalova V; Machova J; Babulova A; Protective action of vinpocetine against experimentally induced gastric damage in rats. Institute of Experimental Pharmacology, Slovak Academy of Sciences, Bratislava. Arzneimittelforschung 1993 Sep;43(9):981-5.

Okuyama S; Hashimoto-Kitsukawa S; Ogawa S; Imagawa Y; Kawashima K; Kawashima Y; Araki H; Otomo S;Effects of VA-045, a novel apovincaminic acid derivative, on age- related impairment evidence in electroencephalograph, caudate spindle, a passive avoidance task and cerebral blood flow in rats. Gen Pharmacol 1994 Nov;25(7): 1311-20

Olpe, H. et al.; "Locus Coeruleus as a target for psychogeriatric agents" Ann NY Acad Sci,1985, 444, 399-405.).

Ordogh, B., Srossy, D., et al.; "Therapeutic Action of Cavinton in Hearing Defects of Neurological Origin". Therapia Hungarica. 1978 ; 26.1:16-9.

Orvisky E; Soltes L; Stancikova M; High-molecular-weight hyaluronan- a valuable tool in testing the antioxidative activity of amphiphilic drugs stobadine and vinpocetine. J Pharm Biomed Anal 1997 Nov;16(3):419-24.

Otomo, E. et al "Comparison of vinpocetine with Ifenprodil Tartrate and Dihyroergotoxine Mesylate treatment and results of long term treatment with vinpocetine." Curr Ther Res (1985) 37, 811-21.

Partanen J; Soininen H; Helkala EL; Kononen M; et al; Relationship between EEG reactivity and neuropsychological tests in vascular dementia. University Hospital of Kuopio, Finland. J Neural Transm 1997;104(8-9):905-12.

Paulo, T. Toth, P.T., et al; (3H) Noradrenaline-releasing action of vinpocetine in the isolated main pulmonary artery of the rabbit. J Pharm. Pharmaacol, (1986) 38, 668-673.

Pudleiner P; Vereczkey L; Study on the absorption of vinpocetine and apovincaminic acid. Chemical Works of Gedeon Richter Ltd, Budapest, Hungary. Eur J Drug Metab Pharmacokinet 1993 Oct-Dec;18(4):317-21.

Ribari, et al; "Ethyl Apovincaminate in the Treatment of Sensorineural Impairment of hearing." Arzneim.-Forsh. (Drug. Res.) 1976, 10. 1977.

Shibuya, T., Sato. K., Effects of vinpocetine on experimental brain ischemia, histological study of brain monomines. Igaku No Ayumi (1986) 139, 3, 217-219.

Silberstein SD; Serotonin (5-HT) and migraine. Comprehensive Headache Center, Germantown Hospital and Medical Center, Philadelphia, PA. Headache 1994 Jul-Aug;34(7):408-1.

Sinclair AJ; Bayer AJ; et al; Altered plasma antioxidant status in subjects with Alzheimer's disease and vascular dementia. Selly Oak Hospital, Birmingham, UK. Int J Geriatr Psychiatry 1998 Dec;13(12):840-5.

Solntseva EI; Bukanova IuV; [Cyclic GMP mimicks potentiation effect of the nootropic agent vinpocetine on the high threshold A-current in the mollusk neurons] Institute of Brain Research, Moscow, Russia. Ross Fiziol Zh Im I M Sechenova 1998 Aug;84(8):741-6.

Solti, F. et al; "Effect of Ethyl Apovincaminate on the cerebral circulation" AF(DR) 1976; 28, 1945-47.

Stancampiano R, et al. Serotonin and acetylcholine release response in the rat hippocampus during a spatial memory task. Neuroscience. 1999;89(4):1135-43.

Stefani MR; Nicholson GM; Gold PE; ATP-sensitive potassium channel blockade enhances spontaneous alternation performance in the rat: a potential mechanism for glucose- mediated memory enhancement. Department of Psychology, University of Virginia, Charlottesville, Neuroscience 1999;93(2):557-63.

Subhan Z; Hindmarch I; Psychopharmacological effects of vinpocetine in normal healthy volunteers. Eur J Clin Pharmacol 1985;28(5):567-71.

Szakall S; Boros I; Balkay L; Emri M; et al; Cerebral effects of a single dose of intravenous vinpocetine in chronic stroke patients: a PET study. Debrecen University Medical School, Hungary. J Neuroimaging 1998 Oct;8(4):197-204.

Tagawa K; Cerebrovascular disorder with memory disturbance, drowsiness, and a lack of drive as major symptoms] Fukuoka Higher Bain Function Center, Nagao Hospital 814-0153 Fukuoka Igaku Zasshi 1998 Nov;89(11):303-11.

Tohgi H; Sasaki K; Chiba K; Nozaki Y; Effect of vinpocetine on oxygen release of hemoglobin and erythrocyte organic polyphosphate concentrations in patients with vascular dementia of the Binswanger type. Department of Neurology, Iwate Medical University, Japan. Arzneimittelforschung 1990 Jun;40(6):640-3.

Tretter L; Adam-Vizi V; The neuroprotective drug vinpocetine prevents veratridine-induced [Na+]i and [Ca2+]i rise in synaptosomes. Department of Medical Biochemistry, Semmelweis University of Medicine, Budapest, Hungary. Neuroreport 1998 Jun 1;9(8):1849-53.

Turrigiano GG; Marder E; Abbott LF; Cellular short-term memory from a slow potassium conductance. Department of Biology, Brandeis University, Waltham, Ma. J Neurophysiol 1996 Feb;75(2):963-6.

Ueyoshi A; Ota K; appraisal of vinpocetine for the removal of intractable tumoral calcinosis in haemodialysis patients with renal failure. J Int Medical Res 1992 Sep;20(5):435-43.

Vamosi, B. et al (1976) "Comparative study of the effect of Ethyl Apovincaminate and Xanthinol Nicotinate in cerebrovascular diseases" Arzneim Forsch (drug research) 28, 1980-84.)

Van Bockstaele EJ; Morphological substrates underlying opioid, epinephrine and gamma-aminobutyric acid inhibitory actions in the rat locus coeruleus. Brain Res Bull 1998 Sep 1;47(1):1-15.

Wei Y; Shi NC; Zhong CS;et al; Inhibitory effects of vinpocetine on sodium current in rat cardiomyocytes. School of Basic Medical Sciences, Shanghai Medical University, China. Chung Kuo Yao Li Hsueh Pao 1997 Sep;18(5):411-5.

Yamada S; Yamaguchi K; Okuyama S;Effects of VA-045 on peripheral and central circulation in anesthetized dogs. Nihon Bioresearch Center Inc., Gifu, Japan. Gen Pharmacol 1995 Oct;26(6):1419-24.

About The Author...

Beth M. Ley, Ph.D., has been a science writer specializing in health and nutrition since 1988 and has written many health-related books, including the best sellers, ***DHEA: Unlocking the Secrets to the Fountain of Youth*** and ***MSM: On Our Way Back to Health With Sulfur***. She wrote her own undergraduate degree program and graduated in Scientific and Technical Writing from North Dakota State University in 1987 (combination of Zoology and Journalism). Dr. Beth has her masters (1998) and doctoral degrees (1999) in Nutrition.

Dr. Beth does Biblical-based nutrition and wellness counseling in Golden Valley, MN, (Twin Cities Area) and also on line (www.blpublications.com). She speaks on Biblical nutrition, health and Divine healing locally and nationwide.

Dr. Beth currently lives in the Minneapolis area. She is dedicated to God and to spreading the health message. She enjoys nature and spending time with her dalmation, KC.

Memberships: American Academy of Anti-aging, New York Academy of Sciences, Oxygen Society and Resurrection Apostolic International Network (RAIN),

Books from BL Publications

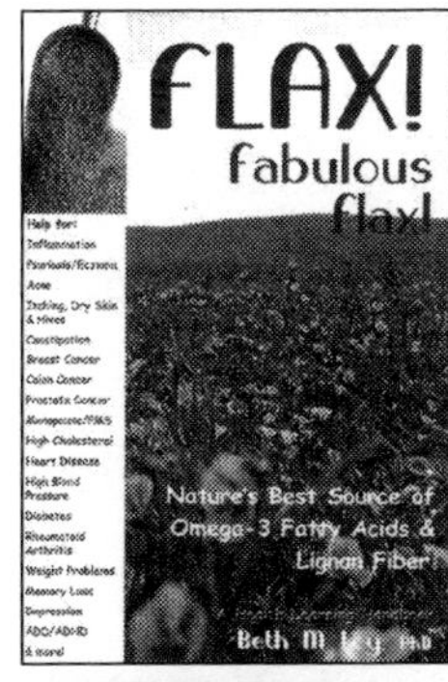

56 pages, $4.95

Spiral Bound Cookbook
200 pages, $19.95

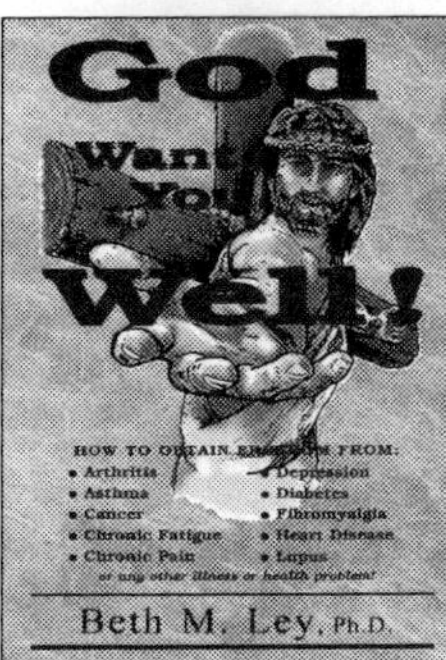

240 pages, $14.95

**Credit card orders
call toll free:
1-877-BOOKS11**

Also visit:
www.blpublications.com

110 pages, $8.95

40 pages, $4.95

120 pgs. $9.95

60 pages, $4.95

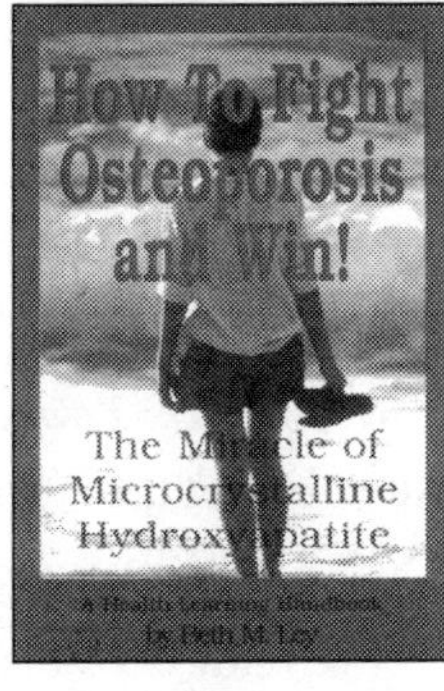

80 pgs. $6.95

<u>T O   P L A C E   A N   O R D E R :</u>

_____ ***Aspirin Alternatives: The Top Natural Pain-Relieving Analgesics*** (Lombardi) $8.95

_____ ***Bilberry & Lutein: The Vision Enhancers!*** (Ley) $4.95

_____ ***Calcium: The Facts, Fossilized Coral*** (Ley) $4.95

_____ ***Castor Oil: Its Healing Properties*** (Ley) $3.95

_____ ***Dr. John Willard on Catalyst Altered Water*** (Ley) $3.95

_____ ***Chlorella: Ultimate Green Food (Ley)*** $4.95

_____ ***CoQ10: All-Around Nutrient for All-Around Health*** (Ley) $4.95

_____ ***Colostrum: Nature's Gift to the Immune System*** (Ley) $5.95

_____ ***DHA: The Magnificent Marine Oil*** (Ley) $6.95

_____ ***DHEA: Unlocking the Secrets/Fountain of Youth-2nd ed.*** (Ash & Ley) $14.95

_____ ***Diabetes to Wholeness*** (Ley) $9.95

_____ ***Discover the Beta Glucan Secret*** (Ley) $3.95

_____ ***Fading: One family's journey ... Alzheimer's*** (Kraft) $12.95

_____ ***Flax! Fabulous Flax!*** (Ley) $4.95

_____ ***Flax Lignans: Fifty Years to Harvest*** (Sönju & Ley) $4.95

_____ ***God Wants You Well*** (Ley) $14.95

_____ ***Health Benefits of Probiotics*** (Dash) $4.95

_____ ***How Did We Get So Fat? 2nd Edition*** (Susser & Ley) $8.95

_____ ***How to Fight Osteoporosis and Win!*** (Ley) $6.95

_____ ***Maca: Adaptogen and Hormone Balancer (Ley)*** $4.95

_____ ***Marvelous Memory Boosters*** (Ley) $3.95

_____ ***Medicinal Mushrooms:*** *Agaricus Blazei Murill (Ley)* $4.95

_____ ***MSM: On Our Way Back to Health W/ Sulfur*** (Ley) SPANISH $3.95

_____ ***MSM: On Our Way Back to Health W/ Sulfur*** (Ley) $4.95

_____ ***Natural Healing Handbook*** (Ley) $14.95

_____ ***Nature's Road to Recovery: Nutritional Supplements for the Alcoholic & Chemical Dependent*** (Ley) $5.95

_____ ***PhytoNutrients: Medicinal Nutrients in Foods***, *Revised /Updated* (Ley) . .$5.95

_____ ***Recipes For Life! (Spiral Bound Cookbook)*** (Ley) $19.95

_____ ***Secrets the Oil Companies Don't Want You to Know*** (LaPointe) $10.00

_____ ***Spewed! How to Cast Out Lukewarm Christianity through Fasting and a Fasted Lifestyle -*** $15.95

_____ ***The Potato Antioxidant: Alpha Lipoic Acid*** (Ley) $6.95

_____ ***Vinpocetine: Revitalize Your Brain w/ Periwinkle Extract!*** (Ley) $5.95

Book subtotal $ ___________ + $5.00 shipping = $________________

Send check or money order to:
BL Publications 649 Kayla Lane, Hanover, MN 55341

Credit card orders please call toll free: 1-877-BOOKS11
For more info visit: www.blpublications.com